How they Work

NUCLEAR-POWERED BALLISTIC MISSILE SUBMARINE

by Frank Vann

Brian Trodd Publishing House

Contents

The SSBN 726 "Ohio" was the first submarine in this class and was commissioned in November 1981.

"Ohio" Class Nuclear-Powered Ballistic-Missile Submarine

The nuclear-powered submarine armed with ballistic missiles is one of the most deadly weapons in service today. It carries an arsenal of armaments which fifty years ago, at the outbreak of World War Two, would have been hard to imagine, so devastating is their power to destroy a whole country, let alone a few cities. The "Ohio" class of submarine is probably the most highly advanced example of these awesome weapon systems. It can hide in the depths of the ocean or under the polar ice-caps, waiting to launch a crippling attack against anyone rash enough to start a war against the United States of America.

As might be expected, the governments of the world are not anxious to reveal too many of the secrets of the design and operation of their nuclear deterrent forces. (Some of the information is "leaked" out, though. If the enemy did not know anything about the nature of the deterrent, he would not be deterred!) As a result, it is not easy to find out many details of the construction of submarines or of how they navigate or launch their missiles.

This book describes what is known about the "Ohio". It also gives a brief history of the scientific research which went into making possible the design and production of such advanced weapon systems. It describes some of the problems which had to be solved before the idea of a nuclear-powered submarine could be turned into a usable system which will play an important part in the future in deterring possible enemies from attacking us.

The fact that nuclear long-range missiles now exist has led to a totally new way of waging major wars. It is to be hoped that the theory will never be put into practice. That terrifying possibility is made less likely if military strategists – that is, the people who plan future wars – think about what might happen and plan to prevent it actually happening.

Modern military thinking is based on the idea of deterrence. That means that an enemy will not be likely to attack us if he knows that his cities will suffer the same appalling destruction as ours when we retaliate by launching our nuclear missiles against him. In other words, he will be deterred from attacking us.

To be successful, the policy of deterrence depends upon the enemy not being able to

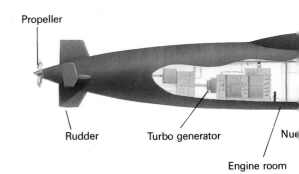

Propeller

Rudder   Turbo generator   Nu(

Engine room

Four members of the crew can be seen standing in the top of the fin of the "Alabama" (SSBN 731) as the submarine cruises on the surface. The 24 missiles are stored beneath the flat deck aft of the fin.

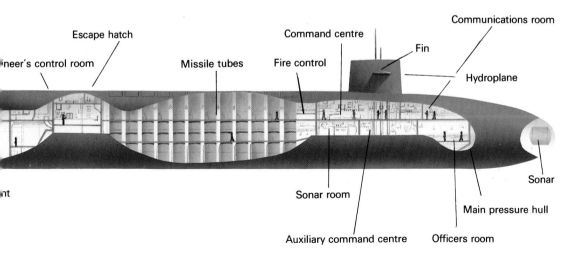

Escape hatch

neer's control room

Missile tubes

Command centre

Fire control

Communications room

Fin

Hydroplane

Sonar room

Auxiliary command centre

Officers room

Main pressure hull

Sonar

nt

Part of the outer shell has been cut away in this side view to reveal the internal layout of the "Ohio" class submarines. The vertical launching tubes in the centre contain the missiles. In front of those are the crew's quarters and the control rooms arranged on a number of floor levels. The aft end is occupied by the nuclear power plant and the engine. The sonar equipment for detecting enemy submarines is right at the front in the nose of the hull.

Water is admitted into the ballast tanks to compel the "Ohio" submarine to sink. By altering the distribution of the water in the tanks along the length of the vessel, the nose can be made

When they are submerged, submarines can be manoeuvred by two different means.

If the weight of the submarine is exactly the same as the amount of water which it displaces, it is in a state of neutral equilibrium and will not have a tendency to rise to the surface or to sink deeper. If it is at rest, it can be made to rise or sink by pumping water out of or into its ballast tanks. If the weight of the vessel is increased by pumping water into the ballast tanks, it will sink down lower in the ocean. If it is lightened by pumping water out of the tanks, it will rise towards the surface.

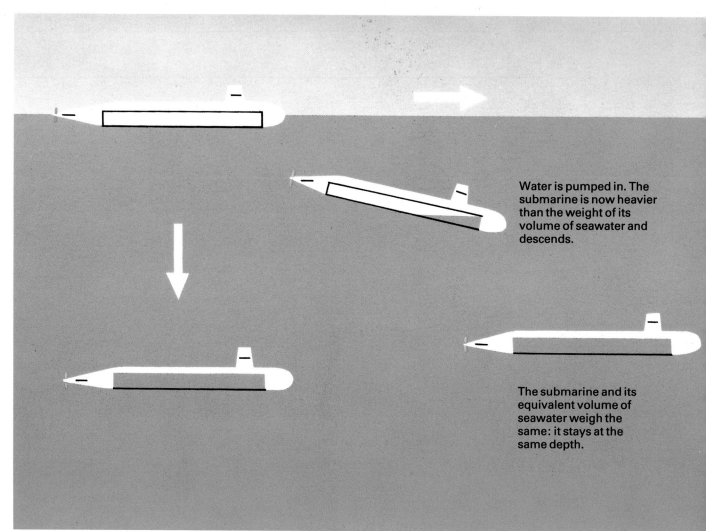

Water is pumped in. The submarine is now heavier than the weight of its volume of seawater and descends.

The submarine and its equivalent volume of seawater weigh the same: it stays at the same depth.

The depth of the submarine can also be controlled dynamically if the vessel is moving forward under the power of its propellor. In that case, the movable control surfaces, the rudder and the horizontal surfaces corresponding to the elevators of an aircraft, can be deflected to produce loads on the sub-marine which propel it sideways or vertically.

By using the first method, the submarine will sink vertically like a stone. The second method enables the captain to dive his vessel to a greater depth in the same way as the pilot of an aircraft controls his machine.

to sink or rise and alter the attitude of the submarine. The inset photograph shows the nose of the submarine emerging from the sea as the captain surfaces at high speed.

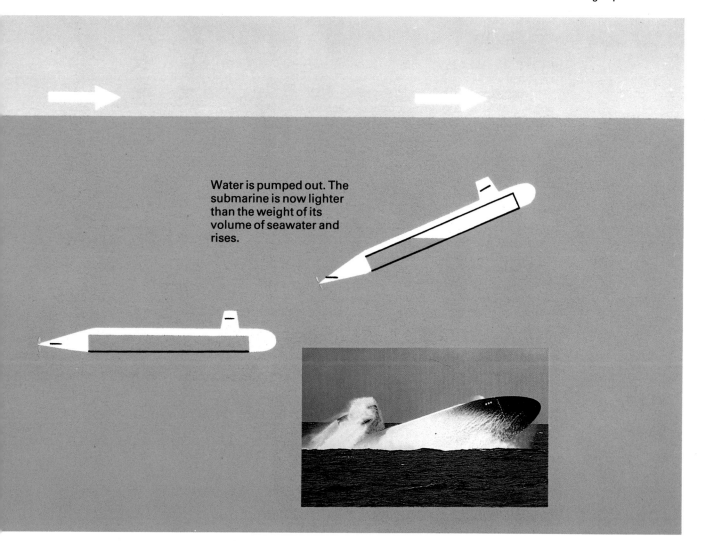

Water is pumped out. The submarine is now lighter than the weight of its volume of seawater and rises.

The mainland of Europe is well within the range of missile-carrying submarines stationed in the North Atlantic. The North polar ice-cap also offers a secure hiding place where submarines can lie undetected for months ready to retaliate against anyone rash enough to attack first.

destroy our missiles before we can strike back. If, in his first unexpected attack, he could knock out all of our missiles before they could be fired, he could attack us with no fear of our retaliating. He would not be deterred.

By the use of modern spy satellites, all of the major powers in the world know exactly where most of their potential enemy's missiles are based. The majority of them are designed to be fired from fixed bunkers whose positions have already been clearly identified.

If war were to come because some enemy power were rash enough to believe that he could defeat us, the first attack would have to be launched against our missile installations to prevent us from firing them back against him. It is very important to prevent this first attack from succeeding if we are not to lose the war in the first hour. Also, the very idea of a deterrent depends on making an enemy believe that it is impossible for him to destroy all of our missiles before we have a chance to launch them. The most important part of our strategy must, therefore, be to preserve our chance to retaliate by making sure that at least some of our missiles survive a first strike by an enemy.

The best way to make our missiles safe against enemy attack is not to keep them in fixed bunkers whose positions are known and where, as has been said, they will be the primary target for an enemy first strike.

One way of doing this is to arrange to fire the missiles not from fixed bases but from moving vehicles. This is the policy adopted with the short-range and medium-range cruise missiles which have been discussed so often in the news of late. The missiles are mounted on large motor vehicles which can be dispersed in the countryside if there is thought to be a real danger that war is likely to break out.

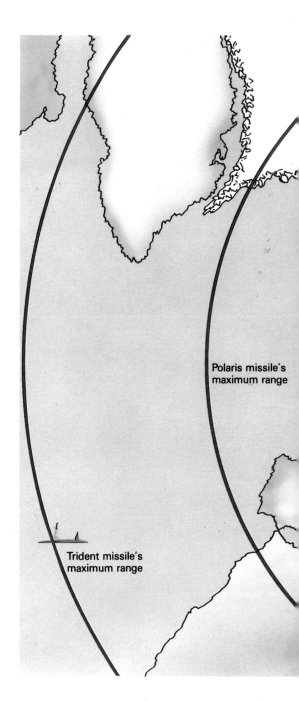

Polaris missile's maximum range

Trident missile's maximum range

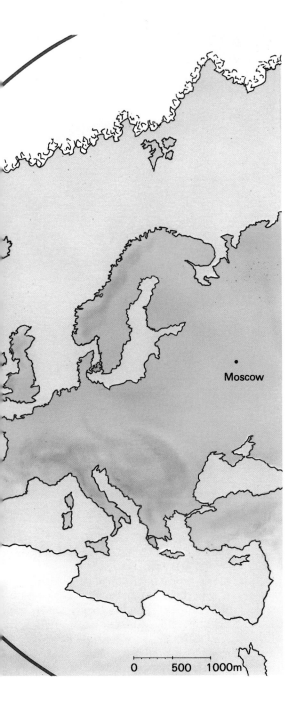

Moscow

0   500   1000m

The theory is that we would always get some indication that an enemy was about to attack us. Perhaps the political situation would be seen to be leading up to a major confrontation. Perhaps our spy satellites would detect warlike preparations in an enemy country showing that he was on the point of launching an attack against us.

If war did seem to become a real possibility, the mobile missiles would be driven away from their bases ready for firing from anywhere at all in the country. This would obviously make it very difficult for an enemy to be sure that he had destroyed all of our missiles in his first strike because he would not know where they were.

In the last World War, it would have been sufficient to destroy less than half of an enemy's forces in an initial attack. Winning or losing a battle depended on establishing a superiority of one's own forces over the enemy. In the end, the victory usually went to the side with the most men, tanks and aircraft engaged in a battle.

The introduction of nuclear weapons has changed all that. If only one enemy missile gets through the defences, a whole city of millions of inhabitants will be wiped out. Destroying even two thirds of an enemy's stock of thousands of missiles will not be enough to ensure that one's own country will survive when he strikes back.

If it is possible, therefore, to devise some system which will make absolutely sure that some of our own missiles will survive the first enemy attack it should be sufficient to deter any potential enemy from attacking us.

Probably the most effective way of doing that is the nuclear-powered submarine capable of firing ballistic missiles.

As we shall see, one modern nuclear-powered submarine carries enough atomic missiles to destroy all the main centres of population in even the largest countries.

An enemy might believe that he had destroyed all of his opponent's submarines. But he could never be sure that he had not missed one. And just that one could launch a devastating attack with nuclear missiles, possibly weeks after he thought that the war was already won.

Why is the submarine the best way of hiding our missiles from sudden attack?

In the first place the oceans cover 71% of the surface of the earth. Their total area amounts to 140 million square miles (360 million square kilometres). So there is a vast amount of space in which a submarine can hide.

The average depth of the oceans is 2,080 fathoms (3,800 metres). It is true that submarines cannot use the full depth of the water to hide in. Even with modern technology, submarines cannot survive at much more than 980 feet (300 metres) below the surface because the pressure of the water is so great that their hulls would be crushed.

Even so, it is not easy to detect submarines when they are submerged at maximum depth, particularly if they close down their engines and lie quietly.

In addition, they can penetrate beneath the polar ice-caps and lie in wait there for weeks.

The exploration of the seas beneath the polar ice-caps started as far back as 1931. In those days, submarines were all powered by diesel engines which could only be used on the surface as they needed air to burn the fuel. When submerged, they had to be driven by electrical power using batteries. So they had to come to the surface frequently to renew the air supply for the crew and to use their diesel engines to charge the batteries.

Also, there were no techniques available for navigating beneath the ice. Nor was there any way of communicating with sub-

marines when they were submerged under water, let alone ice.

All of these problems had to be solved before the submarine could become a successful method of deterring an enemy without itself being destroyed first.

In 1931, a United States submarine named *Nautilus* made the first attempts to penetrate the ice cap surrounding the North Pole.

A submarine breaks through the ice and surfaces in the bleak Arctic. Even the polar wastes offer a welcome change of scenery to the crew after their long confinement below decks.

The boat was fitted with what were in effect inverted skates on the top of the hull. The idea was that if the submarine were made buoyant it would rise up against the bottom of the ice. When its motors were started it would slide along the roof of ice and, in this manner, it could make its way along as near to the surface as possible.

The experiment had only limited success.

The grinding noises made by the "skates" as they slid under the ice frightened the crew. It sounded as if the hull was being torn apart. The bottom of the ice was not flat and smooth but resembled an inverted range of mountains so that the submarine was always hitting some obstruction in its path.

However, the *Nautilus* did make a lot of useful measurements of the conditions under

the ice. These formed the basis of later, more complete knowledge of the environment under the polar ice-caps.

Further experiments were carried out by other submarines in the years leading up to the Second World War. Apart from measuring currents in the sub-polar ocean and the water temperatures existing there, various attempts were made to surface through the ice at suitable points.

The tests started again in 1947 after the war. Another United States submarine, named *Boarfish,* successfully navigated under the polar ice. The *Boarfish* was powered by diesel engines. It was equipped with three

sonar detectors which pointed upwards, downwards and forwards. Sonars radiate sound waves into the water. If they hit a solid object such as another submarine or the bottom of an iceberg, the sound waves are reflected back. Because the speed of sound in water is known, the time between the pulse being emitted and the echo returning can be used to calculate how far away the solid object is. Surface ships use sonar to locate submarines.

With its upward and downward-looking sonars, the *Boarfish* could determine how far above the seabed and how far below the bottom of the ice it was. If there was enough

space available, it could then travel comfortably somewhere in between. The forward-looking sonar told it whether there was an obstacle ahead such as the bottom of a very large iceberg.

From these simple beginnings, a usable technique was developed which formed the basis for the navigation of submarines under the ice-fields near to the poles.

At that time the biggest disadvantage with submarines was that they had diesel engines. As was said earlier, that meant that they still had to surface regularly in whatever open water they could find in order to recharge their batteries and take on a fresh supply of air for the crew to breathe.

The next major advance was the appearance in 1957 of the first submarine powered by a nuclear engine. It was given the name *Nautilus*.

The new *Nautilus* had five sonars pointing upwards so that it could get a rough idea of the shape of the bottom of the ice under which it was passing.

In 1957, *Nautilus* managed to sail 962 miles (1,550 kilometres) under the ice at an average speed of 13 knots. The total time that it was submerged was 74 hours.

Nautilus penetrated under the ice until it was only about 180 miles (290 kilometres) from the North Pole.

Following on from these successes, *Nautilus* and another nuclear-powered submarine, called *Skate*, were sent out in 1958 to cross under the North polar ice-cap from two different directions. By that time, new and much more accurate navigation equipment was available. Both submarines were fitted with inertial navigation systems which are explained in more detail later.

On 3 August 1958, *Nautilus* reached the North Pole by navigating under the ice. At the same time, *Skate* was crossing the ice-cap on a different route starting from Spitz-

Buried under layers of snow, very little of this submarine is to be seen after it has surfaced through the ice.

Jagged blocks of ice surround the fin of a submarine as it forces its way up through the polar ice-cap.

This diagram shows
the top of the world
flattened with the
polar ice-field
separating Europe and
North America. The
latest nuclear
submarines fire
intercontinental missiles
which can reach
almost all of the land
shown when they are
launched from the
polar ice-cap. Only the
Southern tips of South
America and South
Africa are out of
range, but they are
within easy reach of
submarines submerged
beneath the Antarctic.

Left inset:
Commander W. R.
Anderson of the USS
Nautilus searches for
a spot deep enough to
submerge safely
underneath the polar
ice.

Right inset: The USS
Nautilus enters New
York harbour after
becoming the first
submarine to travel
beneath the North
Pole in 1958.

bergen in Norway.

At last it looked as if the main problems of operating submarines under the ice had been solved.

Ships on the surface of the sea used to have to navigate by a combination of dead reckoning and by the use of a sextant and an accurate clock to determine their position. In these days they can also use radar to measure their distance from known pieces of land.

The submarine cannot use radar unless it is willing to surface and risk giving its position away to the enemy. It has difficulty in using the sun or the stars to make astronomical observations to determine its position because it cannot always stay long enough on the surface to take the necessary measurements.

It can use dead reckoning by plotting its course and measuring its speed all the time. But the ocean currents may carry it off its intended course and there is no way of allowing for that without any external measurements.

These problems can be solved by the use of inertial navigation.

It is not difficult for a submarine to measure its speed relative to the water which surrounds it. It is difficult for it to measure its speed relative to the surface of the earth because the water itself is moving.

Without outside observations, it is difficult to know the position of the submarine relative to any fixed point on the surface of the earth except on the day when it starts its voyage. Then, at least, the position of its naval base on the globe is known.

But, with modern technology, it is comparatively easy to measure the acceleration of the submarine in space.

Acceleration is the rate at which the speed is changing with time.

For example, if a car can start from rest

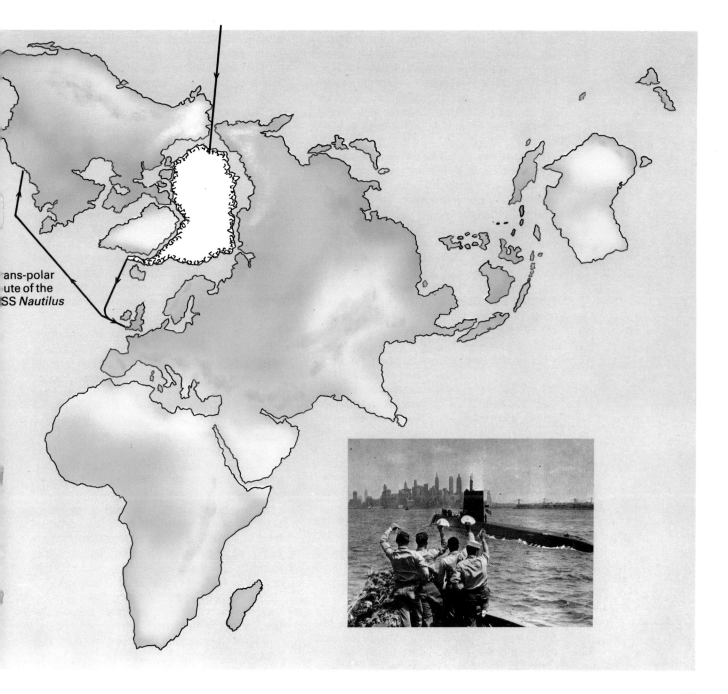

Trans-polar
route of the
USS *Nautilus*

and reach a speed of 3 feet per second in one second, we say that its acceleration is 3 feet per second per second. If, on the other hand, it takes 2 seconds to reach a speed of 40 feet per second, its acceleration is 20 feet per second per second, because it is increasing its speed by 20 feet per second in every second.

A submarine or any other vehicle starts at a known time from a known location. Using accurate instruments, we can measure the variation of the acceleration of the vehicle with time. This gives us a complete history of acceleration and time since the start of the journey.

With the help of a mathematical process known as integration, it is quite easy to use the accelerations to calculate the variation of speed of the vehicle over the same period of time. If we then integrate the speed of the vehicle over that time interval, we get the distance travelled.

To do that, we need to measure the acceleration very accurately. Any small error in the measurement of the acceleration will be magnified in each of the two integration processes and produce inaccurate answers.

Today there are extremely accurate ways of measuring accelerations by using very precise instruments known as accelerometers. There are also electronic computers to do all the integration calculations very quickly.

As a result, if the submarine knows the time at which it left a fixed point on the Earth's surface, such as its naval base, it knows at any time afterwards where it is relative to that point.

Because the submarine is not going to move along a straight line for the whole of its travels, it is necessary to measure the accelerations in three directions all at right angles to each other. This means that the computer can tell the captain where the submarine is relative to its starting point in all three dimensions.

The inertia of a body is its resistance to being accelerated. For that reason the process is known as inertial navigation.

That is a very simple explanation of how submarines can determine their position by measuring their acceleration. In practice it is a much more complicated process, but the principle is basically as stated.

One problem is that the inertial navigation system is working out the position of the submarine in space. Because the Earth is turning under the submarine, an allowance has to be made for that when calculating the position of the submarine relative to a fixed point of the Earth. The fixed point is not where it was in space when the submarine left it. These effects have to be included in the computer program.

The big advantage of inertial navigation is that it does not depend on any information obtained from outside the submarine. Therefore, it cannot be detected and, more important still, it cannot be jammed by the enemy.

The accelerometers have to be made to the most precise dimensions to get the accuracy needed. As a result they are very expensive to make.

Gyroscopes also have to be included in the system to determine the directions of the accelerations.

If you have ever played with a toy gyroscope, you will know that it always wants to keep the axis about which it rotates pointing in the same direction. If an attempt is made to disturb it, it moves in a direction at right angles to the way in which it is pushed.

This property of the gyroscope can be used to determine the direction in which a body is trying to move.

Gyroscopes for use in navigation often still depend on spinning flywheels for their operation in the same way as the toy gyroscope.

19

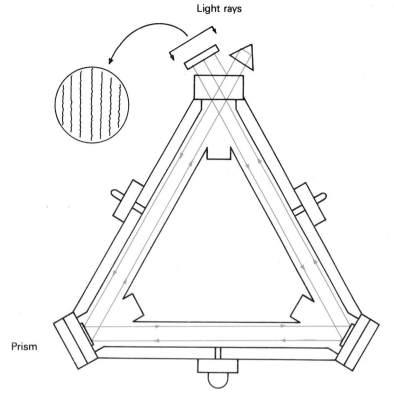

Light rays

Prism

The main problem is in keeping the friction in their bearings to as low a level as possible. Many ingenious devices have been invented for this purpose. Some have the rotating axles supported on a tiny bed of air. Others have them suspended in space by electrostatic forces.

The most modern development in gyroscopes is the ring laser gyro. In this, the rotating flywheels are replaced by beams of light travelling around a triangle of mirrors.

The beams of light are directed round the mirrors in opposite directions. If the mirrors are still, the light will take the same time to go round both ways.

However, if the mirrors are moving, the light will take a very tiny fraction of a millisecond longer to go round one way than the other. This is because while the light is on its way from one mirror to the next, the mirrors will have changed position due to the motion of the vehicle in which the gyro is

mounted. Thus, one beam of light will have to travel a shorter path because the next mirror is coming to meet it. The beam of light going in the other direction will have further to go because its next mirror is moving away from it.

If you consider that the speed of light is almost 186,000 miles (300,000 kilometres) per second and that the paths of the light beams are measured in fractions of metres, it becomes obvious that very accurate measurements of time are required to get any sensible result at all from the ring laser gyro.

Modern technology using computers can solve such problems of accurate measurements. The ring laser gyro is now a standard piece of equipment on many modern vehicles which are steered by inertial navigation. This includes submarines.

So we now can see that the problem of navigation has been solved by the inertial guidance system. The problem that the submarine has in needing to surface frequently to take in fresh air has been solved by the nuclear-powered engine, which also gives much extended range and allows the submarine to stay away from its base for a much longer time.

The remaining problem is that of communicating with the submarine, particularly when it is submerged. It is one thing to talk to a submarine once a day to give it general instructions about its tactics, as was the practice in the Second World War. It is quite another when the message to be transmitted is an order to launch its arsenal of nuclear missiles. In that case the system must be absolutely foolproof. The message must be received at exactly the right time so that the submarine's response is co-ordinated with other actions in other parts of the world. There is no room for misunderstandings or doubts about what was actually said.

The principle of the ring laser gyro is shown very simply in this diagram. The beam of light travels round its triangular path in one direction before being reflected back in the other direction by a prism. Because of the motion of the whole instrument, the light takes a different time to go in each of the two directions. This difference in time shows up as a phase difference between the returning light beam and the original outgoing beam. The phase difference can be used to measure the speed of the vehicle containing the ring laser gyro.

SSBN 727 "Michigan" lying on the surface of a relatively calm sea.

Acceleration, Velocity and Distance

Distance is a very easy idea to understand. We all realise that a one mile walk is not hard but a 50 mile walk is very difficult unless you are an athlete.

Velocity or speed is the rate at which distance changes with time. For example, if your car can travel a distance of 30 miles in a time of half an hour, you would agree that its speed is 60 miles an hour. If we think about it the other way round, we can work out the distance travelled if we know the speed and the time taken to complete the journey. For instance, if you travel at a speed of 60 miles an hour for a time of two hours, it is not difficult to come to the conclusion that you would cover a distance of 120 miles on the journey.

Acceleration is a bit more difficult to understand. Acceleration is the rate at which the speed changes with time. Again, let us start from the change in speed in order to calculate the acceleration. Our car is travelling at a speed of 60 feet per second. The driver wants to go faster so he presses down on the accelerator and, as a result, 10 seconds later our speed has increased to 70 feet per sec. The speed has increased by 10 feet per second in a time of 10 seconds, so we can say that the acceleration has been 1 foot per second in every second. The physicist would say that the acceleration was 1 foot per second per second.

We can also do that calculation the other way round so that, if we know the acceleration and the length of time that it has been acting, we can calculate the speed. For instance, if our car accelerates at 5 feet per second per second for 10 seconds, its speed will increase by 50 feet per second. Once we know its speed we can calculate the distance that it has travelled in a given time.

That is a very simple explanation of how, by measuring accurately the acceleration of a vehicle and the elapsed time, it is possible to calculate the distance that a vehicle has travelled.

Engineers and physicists like to represent these ideas by using graphs. Graphs are just a way of making pictures of mathematical processes. The graphs on this page show a typical variation of acceleration, speed and

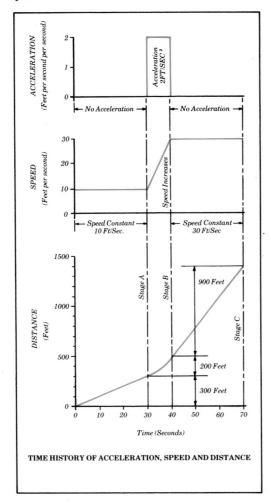

TIME HISTORY OF ACCELERATION, SPEED AND DISTANCE

distance plotted against the time involved.

In this case, at the beginning of our graph on the left hand side, the submarine is travelling at a constant speed of 10 feet per second. Its acceleration is zero because its speed is not changing. It continues like that for 30 seconds in which time it travels 300 feet.

At stage A (30 seconds from the beginning), the captain decides to increase his speed, that is, to accelerate. He increases the power from his engines and the submarine accelerates at a rate of 2 feet per second per second for 10 seconds. At the end of that 10 seconds the speed of the submarine will have increased by 2 feet per second per second in every one of the 10 seconds. That is, the speed has increased in total by 20 feet per second. At stage B, therefore, its speed is now the original 10 feet per second plus the increase of 20 feet per second making a new speed of 30 feet per second.

It is a bit more difficult to calculate how far the submarine has travelled in that time because its speed was continually increasing. Its average speed was 20 feet per second, so in the 10 seconds it travelled another 200 feet. By stage B, therefore, the total distance that it has moved since the beginning is 300 feet (up to stage A) plus 200 feet (from A to B), making a total of 500 feet.

At stage B, the captain decides that he is going fast enough so he stops accelerating and keeps the speed constant at 30 feet per second. The acceleration is now zero again because the speed is not changing. The distance travelled is increasing at 30 feet per second so the line representing distance on the graph is again straight and the distance is increasing linearly with time.

At stage C, 30 seconds after stage B, the acceleration is zero, the speed is 30 feet per second and the distance travelled since stage B is 900 feet, making a total distance since the beginning of 1400 feet.

The USS *City of Corpus Christi* (SSN 705) is shown travelling along the ocean's surface at a high rate of velocity. It is only while submerged that a submarine has to rely on inertial navigation.

The Ohio submarine trails an aerial to pick up the very low frequency radio signals which enable it to receive instructions from home.

The most obvious way of communicating with a submarine at long distances from its base is by radio.

Unfortunately, radio waves are not very efficient at penetrating water. So, when the submarine is submerged, it is not possible to contact it directly with the type of radio transmission used to communicate with surface ships or aircraft.

Experiments showed that the ability of radio waves to penetrate water varied with the frequency and, therefore, with the wavelength. (The wave-length multiplied by the frequency is a constant value and is equal to the speed of light). In other words, low frequency waves are very long and high frequency waves are short.

It was found that high frequency radio waves were quickly absorbed by the water and could not be picked up by a submarine. Lower frequency waves could penetrate deeper below the surface.

Further experiments were carried out which demonstrated that it was possible to establish radio communication with submarines by using very low frequency (VLF) radio transmissions. The VLF radio operates in the frequency range of 3 kHz to 30 kHz (3,000 to 30,000 cycles per second).

One such system was given the code name TACAMO. The transmitter was housed in a large aircraft which had to circle while it trailed an aerial 6 miles (10 kilometres) long hanging vertically. The aerial was used to transmit very powerful VLF signals. This was obviously not a practical way of talking to a submarine in wartime conditions.

In order to pick up the transmissions, the submerged submarine had to trail a buoy containing a suitable aerial at a depth of not more than 20 feet (6 metres) below the surface of the sea which would make the submarine easier to detect by enemy forces.

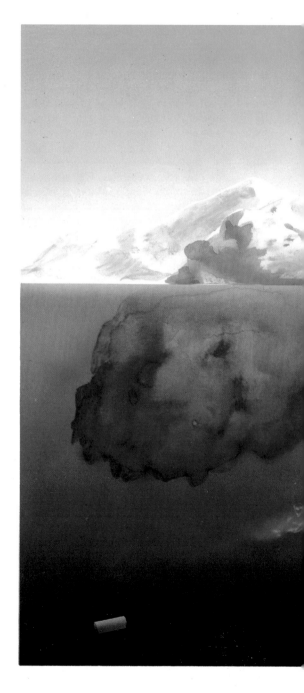

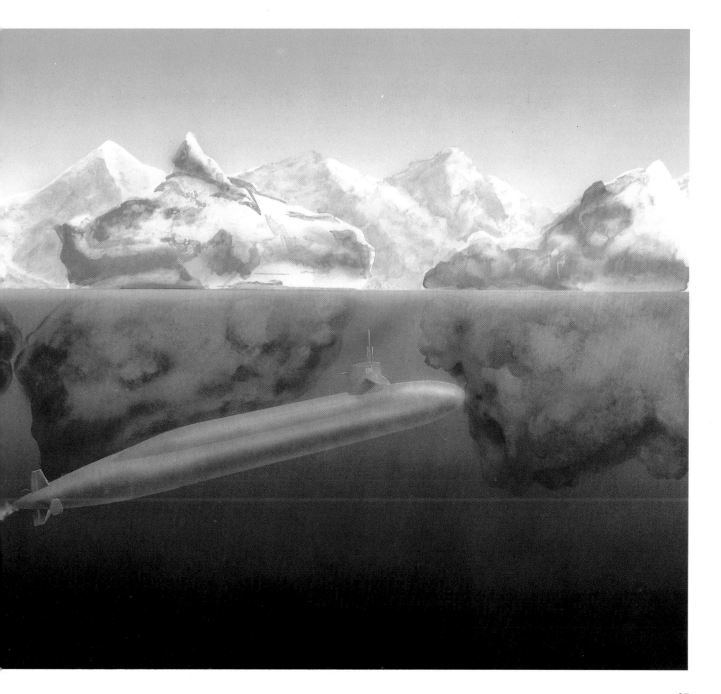

On the left of the picture is the land-based ELF radio station which can communicate with submarines even when they are deeply submerged. Signals can also be transmitted to submarines from aircraft, satellites and surface ships.

This requirement led to the development of the use of extremely low frequency (ELF) radio transmissions. These lie in the frequency range of 30 Hz to 3 kHz (30 to 3,000 cycles per second).

Using ELF, it is possible to communicate with submarines even when they are submerged very deeply.

Because the frequency of ELF is very low, it follows that the wave length must be very high. In fact, it is many thousands of kilometres.

For the most efficient transmission of radio waves, the aerial should be the same length as the wave length corresponding to the frequency being used. This means that the ELF transmitting aerial should also be thousands of kilometres long. If room could be found to construct such a large aerial, it would be easy to destroy by nuclear or conventional attack before it could be used in a war.

By folding up the aerial array in a rectangular pattern, the ground area can be considerably reduced. The United States Government first built an aerial of that type in Wisconsin.

The ground on which it stands has to form part of the aerial system. As a result, only ground which has certain electrical properties can be used as a site for such aerials. This limits the choice of possible sites for building a workable system.

Such aerials are very directional, that is, they transmit their strongest signal in one direction only. It is necessary, therefore, to build two antennae at right angles to each other to give a wide reception area for the transmissions. The Wisconsin aerial is built on this principle and covers a large square area. It is 14 miles (23 kilometres) across.

A prime advantage of ELF is that, unlike systems using the more usual higher frequencies, it is impossible to jam and it is not

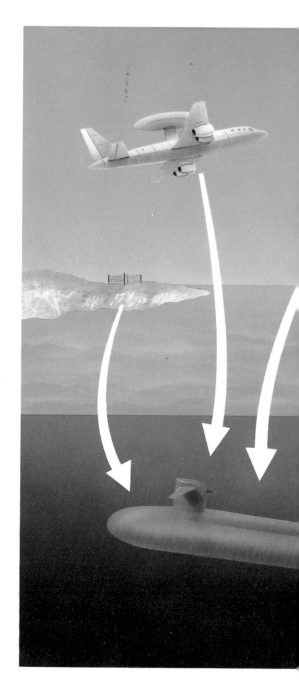

destroyed by the huge electronic impulses caused by nuclear explosions.

It was also found that one aerial was sufficient to transmit radio messages to any part of the whole world. This is because the radio waves become more or less trapped in the atmosphere and are deflected around the curvature of the Earth.

In order to receive the signal, the submarine has to trail an aerial about 2,000 feet (600 metres) long, but does not need to come up to the surface to do this. It can still receive signals when it is submerged at a depth of 300 feet (100 metres).

The long aerial is streamed so far behind the submarine in order to get it away from the submarine's own noise field. Otherwise, it would be difficult to pick up the relatively weak ELF signals penetrating the water above the submarine.

The one disadvantage with ELF is the fact that it takes a long time to transmit anything but the shortest message because the frequency is so low.

The problem is that, as so often in scientific research, there are two requirements which cannot be satisfied at the same time. If we use ELF radio, it will take a long time to transmit a message. If we use a higher frequency it will limit the depth below the surface at which the submarine can pick up the signals. The best compromise has to be found which gives a workable system.

The United States Navy now has two more ELF transmitters working in Michigan and Wisconsin. The antenna of the Wisconsin station is 28 miles (45 kilometres) long. That at Michigan is 56 miles (90 kilometres) long. Presumably, they are of different sizes because they transmit different frequencies.

The situation today is that, after years of scientific research and experiment, the main problems involved in the operation of submarines have been solved.

This photograph was taken during the construction of SSBN 727 "Michigan" one of the Ohio class submarines. Prior to the launch, the vessel is encumbered with an assortment of false-work, fixtures and decking which are needed for the construction phase but which will be removed as soon as the submarine is launched.

It is possible to build submarines which can stay submerged for many weeks.

The submarines can determine their position accurately by using inertial guidance without any reference to the outside world and without giving away their presence.

They can receive instructions from their base without coming to the surface to communicate.

Most importantly of all from the point of view of an effective deterrent to possible attackers, they can carry long-range nuclear missiles with multiple warheads capable of destroying several targets in enemy territory in one attack.

Among the most effective of these submarines in service today are the "Ohio" class boats of the United States Navy. They are impressive because of their size, which is greater than that of any other submarine except for the "Typhoon" class submarines of the Soviet Russian Navy.

The reason why they need to be so big is that they carry 24 launching tubes each containing a Trident ballistic missile. These missiles, as will be seen, are very large rockets over 32 feet (10 metres) long and weighing many tonnes.

As a protection against enemy submarines, the "Ohio" also carries anti-submarine torpedoes.

In addition, so that it can stay submerged for weeks, the submarine has a nuclear-powered engine. The engines in themselves are very large and very heavy because of the weight of the shielding which surrounds them to protect the crew from the harmful effects of radiation from the nuclear fuel.

The "Ohio" carries two complete crews who alternately take over the responsibility for operating the submarine. Altogether the full complement of personnel amounts to over 130 men. These all have to be accommodated on board, together with

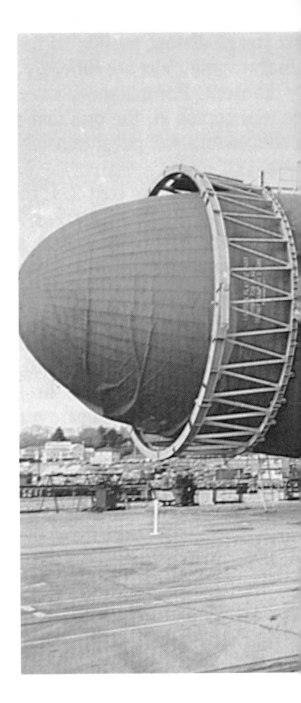

The size of modern submarines is clearly illustrated by this diagram. On the left is an American football pitch. The lowest view shows an Ohio class submarine which is roughly one and a half times the length of the football pitch. Even larger versions of Russian submarines, such as those in the Typhoon class, are in service with the Russian Navy. They exceed the size of even the Ohio class ships.

enough food and drink to last them for the whole voyage.

In order to be able to navigate accurately while submerged, the "Ohio" has to carry a large quantity of very sophisticated navigation equipment which can fix the submarine's position by the use of inertial navigation systems as described earlier. They can also take data from navigational satellites orbiting the Earth.

As a result of all these requirements, the "Ohio" is very large indeed. It is 560 feet (171 metres) long. If you can imagine the

length of 1½ American Football Pitches you will realise how massive is the "Ohio" submarine.

Its width is nearly 42 feet (13 metres) and it needs a depth of water of almost 36 feet (11 metres) just to float in.

When it is floating on the surface of the sea, its displacement is almost 17,000 tonnes. When it is submerged, it displaces 18,700 tonnes.

Its maximum speed is a secret but it is believed to be about 30 knots.

When they are submerged, submarines

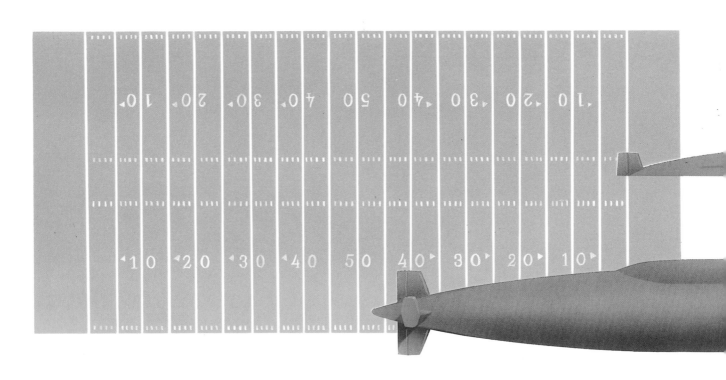

can be manoeuvred by two different means.

If the weight of the submarine is exactly the same as the amount of water which it displaces, it is in a state of neutral equilibrium and will not have a tendency to rise to the surface or to sink deeper. If it is at rest, it can be made to rise or sink by pumping water out of or into the ballast tanks. If the weight of the vessel is increased by pumping water into the ballast tanks, it will sink down lower in the ocean. If it is lightened by pumping water out of the tanks, it will rise towards the surface.

The depth of the submarine can also be controlled dynamically if the vessel is moving forward under the power of its propellor. In that case, the movable control surfaces, the rudder and the horizontal surfaces corresponding to the elevators of an aircraft, can be deflected to produce loads on the submarine which propel it sideways or vertically.

By using the first method, the submarine will sink vertically like a stone. The second method enables the captain to dive his vessel to a greater depth in the same way as the pilot of an aircraft controls his machine.

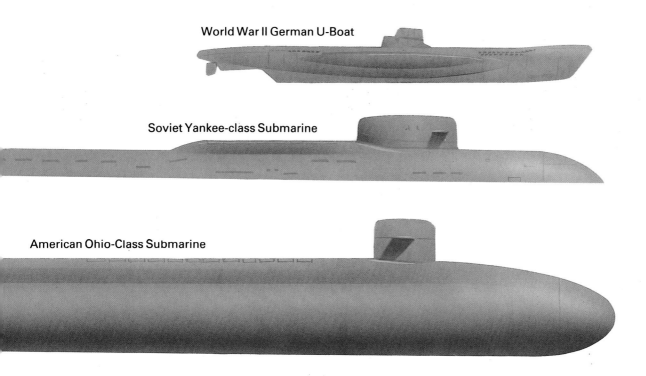

World War II German U-Boat

Soviet Yankee-class Submarine

American Ohio-Class Submarine

A submarine is only comparatively safe as long as it is submerged. Every time it has to come to the surface for any reason, whether it is to use its periscope, to operate its radar or to get a fresh supply of air, it is making itself easy to detect. For that reason, the "Ohio" is designed to spend very long periods of time submerged.

It can operate at depths of down to 980 feet (300 metres). At that depth the water pressure on the hull is about 30 bars (425 lb/sq in). As the submarine is 560 feet long and up to 42 feet wide at its broadest part, its total area in plan view is about 22,000 square feet. So the load which is trying to crush it flat due to water pressure is of the order of 600,000 tonnes! It is no wonder that the structure of the hull has to be made so heavy.

The easiest way for an enemy to detect a submarine is by listening for the noise that it makes. The instruments used for this are known as hydrophones.

The designers of the "Ohio" submarines have gone to great lengths to reduce the noise that the engines make when they are running. All the moving parts of the propulsion system which produce noise are mounted on a bed-plate. This is supported on specially designed mountings which absorb any vibration before it reaches the hull and prevent it being transmitted into the water.

As can be seen from this illustration, the crew's quarters in a modern submarine are more spacious than most of us would imagine. There is enough space for a dining room where the crew can eat in comfortable surroundings.

A cat-walk has been installed on the deck of this submarine to make it easier for workers to arry out servicing operations.

33

History

There are at present eight submarines of the *Ohio* class in service. All the submarines of that class were named after states of the USA. The first of the series to be built was given the name "Ohio" when it was commissioned and that name has been used ever since to refer to all that type of boat.

The early history of this class of submarine was one of delay and indecision. The first boat was three years late to the original programme. It was laid down in the April of 1976 and launched almost exactly three years later on 7 April 1979.

It was built by General Dynamics (Electric Boat Division) in Groton, Connecticut, in the United States of America.

All of the other seven submarines in service have been built by the same manufacturer. Two more have been launched and another should make its appearance in 1988. One of the two which have already been launched is due to go into service in December 1988.

The eight submarines in service at the present time are numbered SSBN 726 to 733 and their names, in that order, are:

SSBN 726	OHIO	SSBN 730	RHODE ISLAND
SSBN 727	MICHIGAN	SSBN 731	ALABAMA
SSBN 728	FLORIDA	SSBN 732	ALASKA
SSBN 729	GEORGIA	SSBN 733	NEVADA

For some reason which is not clear, the *Rhode Island* had its name changed later to *Henry M. Jackson*.

As far as is known, it is intended to build 17 submarines of this class in total. The later boats will be equipped with improved versions of the Trident missile with increased range and bigger warheads.

On average, the United States Government is releasing enough money to build one submarine each year until about 1992.

SSBN 727 "Michigan" almost ready for launching. The lids covering the six most aft missile launching tubes can be seen open in this photograph.

The *Ohio* was three years being built and entered service two and a half years after it was launched. The latest information available shows that the *Alaska* and the *Nevada* took only two years to build and entered service two years after their launching.

As was said earlier, information on the internal arrangements of these submarines is very difficult to find.

Based on what is known about earlier submarines with nuclear-powered engines it is reasonable to assume that the lay-out is as follows:

The engines will be right at the rear end of the hull so that the length of the shaft driving the single propeller is as short as possible. The power unit consists of steam turbines which are duplicated so that the submarine is still operational with one engine failed. Each of the turbines can produce 30,000 horse-power. The total power of 60,000 horse-power is capable of producing a speed of over 25 knots, but the true figure is not available to the public.

Immediately in front of the engines will be the nuclear reactor which produces the heat to generate steam for the turbines. The type used on the "Ohio" is a General Electric pressurised water-cooled reactor.

In the centre of the submarine will be located the 24 launching tubes for the Trident missiles. The tubes are arranged in 12 rows, each row containing a pair of tubes. These can be used to launch the missiles while the submarine is submerged. More details are given later in this book in the description of the missiles themselves.

One advantage of having the missiles in the centre of the boat is that the centre of gravity of the submarine is not too much affected when they are launched. Another is that they separate the crew in the front end from the nuclear reactor at the aft end. The crew are thus protected from being exposed

to any stray nuclear radiation from the reactor.

Forward of the missiles will be the crew's quarters and the control room located beneath the fin protruding from the top of the hull. The crew are accommodated on four decks, beneath which are the electrical storage batteries.

Right at the front end in the bows are the sonars used for detecting other vessels which may be hostile. The only weapons

SSBN 727 "Michigan" being towed into the Naval Submarine Base at Bangor in the state of Washington. The network of cables around the basin is used to neutralise any magnetic field in the hull and make the submarine less liable to detection. Similar systems were used during World War Two to prevent merchant ships from activating magnetic mines.

which the submarine carries apart from its Trident missiles are its torpedoes. On the "Ohio" there are four 21-inch (530-mm) torpedo tubes.

As we saw, the "Ohio" is designed so that it needs the minimum of servicing and maintenance. It stays at sea for a period of about 70 days without returning to port. Because it carries two complete crews, it is operational for the whole of that time.

After each 70-day spell of duty, it has to spend 25 days in port while it is prepared for its next voyage.

Every nine years it has to have a major overhaul to renew the nuclear fuel in its engines.

The first eight submarines of the "Ohio" class are to be based at Bangor in the state of Washington, on the north-west coast of the USA.

It is believed that later ones will operate from King's Bar in the state of Georgia.

Armament

The prime purpose of the "Ohio" class of submarines is to launch "Trident" underwater-to-surface ballistic missiles.

As we have already seen, the submarine carries 24 missiles in launching tubes mounted vertically in the hull. Circular hinged caps seal off the tops of the tubes until they are to be fired.

The first eight "Ohio" class submarines are armed with Trident I C-4 missiles.

The missiles can be launched when the submarine is on the surface or when it is completely submerged.

When the order is given to launch one or more missiles, compressed gas is admitted into the appropriate launching tubes. As it expands, it forces the missile upwards out of the tube.

The solid fuel rocket motor does not ignite until the missile is at a safe distance from the submarine. Then the first-stage motor ignites to start the boost phase of the launch.

Installed in the nose of the missile is a spike with a circular disc at its front end which extends at this stage of the launch. It improves the aerodynamic performance of the missile by guiding the air round the nose of the missile, reducing its drag and making it more stable in flight.

The second stage begins when the first-stage motor burns out because all of the solid fuel is exhausted. The empty motor casing and the part of the missile structure which supports it are separated from the rest of the missile and abandoned.

The second-stage solid fuel rocket motor then ignites to continue the boost phase of the launch.

When that motor burns out, it is separated in turn as the first-stage motor was previously.

An Ohio class
submarine launches
one of its missiles
while it is still deeply
submerged.

This view looking
forward along the
upper side of USS
Ohio shows the covers
of the Trident missile
launching tubes open.
After each patrol, the
missiles are removed
for servicing.

The third-stage motor then ignites to complete the boost phase.

When that motor finally burns out, the missile should be on course for its target at the correct altitude and speed.

The Trident C-4 missile does not carry only a single nuclear warhead. It is equipped with eight separate warheads which can be directed to eight individual targets.

The task of targetting the eight warheads is performed by the post-boost control system.

This ensures that all of the warheads are released in the right directions with the correct velocities to hit their targets.

The missile has an inertial guidance system which works in the way described earlier for the submarine. The fire control subsystem in the submarine inputs information to the missile before it is launched, to tell it where it is starting from and where it is aiming for. The computer in the missile then uses the measurements from the inertial guidance system to correct the flight path to the target.

The range of the Trident is about 4,700 miles (7,500 kilometres) but its guidance system is so accurate that the warhead will hit the target within an error of 500 yards (460 metres). This accuracy is only possible if the submarine knows its own position to the same degree of accuracy at the moment when the missile is launched.

So that any errors will not seriously affect the accuracy of the warhead's aiming, the Trident post-boost vehicle (PBV) has a stellar sensor. When the boost phase is finished and the PBV is ready to deploy the warheads, the stellar sensor checks the position of certain selected stars. If they are not where the sensor expected them to be, that indicates some inaccuracy in the guidance of the missile up to that point. The PBV then takes corrective action by adjusting the

Page 42:
The container shown in this photograph is used for the handling of Trident I C-4 missiles. The picture shows a missile being loaded into a launch tube of SSBN 726 "Ohio".

Page 43 left:
A rare view of the interior of the missile compartment of SSBN 726 Ohio. On each side can be seen the enormous tubes housing the intercontinental nuclear missiles.

Page 43 right:
A Trident missile blasts off on its deadly journey from below the surface of the ocean.

speed or direction of the war-heads to ensure that they hit their targets.

The amount of calculation needed to handle all the data involved was so enormous that new computers had to be designed to cope with it. The Trident Digital Control Computer (TDCC) was designed to provide the data which the missile had to receive before it was launched, so that it would know where it was starting from and where it was going.

The digital read-in sub-system (DRISS) is used by the TDCC to turn all the analogue outputs obtained from the navigation systems and the optical readings into a digital form which the computer can process.

As the Trident has three boost stages, it is a big missile. It is 34 feet (10.39 metres) long. Its outer shell is 6 ft 2 in (1.88 metres) in diameter. When it is launched, it weighs 65,000 lb (29,500 kg).

From the outset, the "Ohio" submarines were designed to carry even bigger versions of the Trident. These will be known as the "Trident II" and will be heavier, have longer range and carry bigger warheads than Trident I.

All "Ohio" class submarines from the ninth onwards will be armed with Trident II when they enter service. The first eight boats will be converted later.

The launch tubes of all the "Ohio" submarines are big enough to take a larger missile but it is not yet clear how this extra room will be used on the Trident II.

It could be employed to include bigger motors to extend the range with the same payload or to achieve the same range with a greater payload.

An effort will certainly be made to improve the accuracy of the missile. A method of correcting the flight-path by checking with satellites orbiting the Earth is certain to be one option.

The weight of the body of the missile will

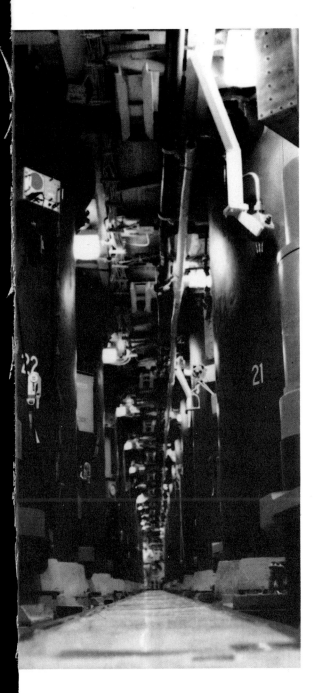

be reduced by the use of carbon fibre composite material (or graphite epoxy, as Americans prefer to call it), instead of metal for some parts of the structure.

The length of the Trident II will be increased to 44 feet (13.42 metres) and its diameter to 6 ft 11 in (2.11 metres).

Its launch weight will be 130,000 lb (59,000 kg).

Each missile will be able to carry up to 15 separately targetable warheads of even greater destructive power than those of Trident I.

It is possible that its range could be extended to more than 6000 nautical miles (11,100 kilometres) so that from the sea it could reach any part of even the largest continent.

Even at that range, it is hoped to be able to drop each warhead within a radius of only 400 feet (120 metres) from its intended target.

As was said at the beginning of this book, the "Ohio" submarine is the most highly-developed weapon of destruction that has yet been invented. It not only represents the most potent attacking force ever installed in one vehicle, but also has an amazing ability to hide itself away from detection by its enemies.

It can lurk beneath the polar ice-caps waiting for the time to launch a devastating attack. It can remain submerged for long periods. It can navigate in the world's oceans without making use of any outside points of reference. It can receive orders by radio from base without having to give away its position by approaching the surface of the ocean.

If any armament is going to be effective in deterring an aggressor from launching a sudden attack against the United States and its allies, surely the "Ohio" nuclear-powered submarine with its ballistic nuclear missiles must, at least for the time being, be the one

Left:
The enemies of the submarine, naval helicopters, prepare to take off from the deck of an aircraft carrier.

Right:
Russian helicopters and attack aircraft line up on the deck of a Soviet aircraft carrier ready to attack hostile submarines.

45

INDEX